My Country
South Africa

Cath Senker

A⁺

Smart Apple Media

Published by Smart Apple Media
P.O. Box 3263, Mankato, Minnesota 56002
www.blackrabbitbooks.com

Published by arrangement with the Watts Publishing
Group LTD, London.

Library of Congress Cataloging-in-Publication Data

Senker, Cath. South Africa / Cath Senker.
p. cm.—(My country)
Summary: "Describes life in South Africa. Readers are
introduced to Mandisa, who tells about the country's
landscape, celebrations, and food. A fast facts page
with information on religion, language, and geography is
included"—Provided by publisher.
Includes index.
ISBN 978-1-59920-907-4 (library binding)
1. South Africa—Juvenile literature. 2. South Africa—
Social life and customs—Juvenile literature. I. Title.
DT1719.S46 2015
968--dc23

2012024751

Series Editor: Paul Rockett
Series Designer: Paul Cherrill for Basement68
Picture Researcher: Diana Morris

Every attempt has been made to clear copyright. Should
there be any inadvertent omission please apply to the
publisher for rectification.

Picture credits: Africa Media Online/Alamy: 11; Arteki /
Shutterstock: 22b; Don Bayley/istockphoto: front cover
c, 4t, 12b, 15b, 18b, 22t; Ecoprint/Shutterstock: 8; Andrew
Esiebo/TwentyTen/Panos: 18t; Fatomousso/Dreamstime:
front cover cl; Focus on Nature/istockphoto: 20; John
Hone/Africa Media Online: 9; Peter Horee/Alamy: 6; Ingrid
Hudson/Eye Ubiquitous/Hutchison: 12t; Instinia Photo/
Dreamstime: 3, 21; meunierd/Shutterstock: 1, 5; Eric Miller/
Panos: 15t, 19; James Oatway/Panos: 16; Cliff Parnell/
istockphoto: 7; Christine Pemberton/Alamy: 13; rambo182/
istockphoto: 4b; Feije Riemersma/Dreamstime: 14, 24b;
Pal Teravagimov/Shutterstock: front cover cr; Peter
Titmuss/Alamy: 17; Micky Wiswedel/istockphoto: 2, 10.

Printed in Stevens Point, Wisconsin at Worzalla
PO 1654
4-2014

9 8 7 6 5 4 3 2 1

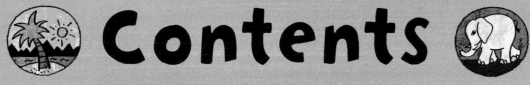 Contents

All words in **bold**
appear in the
glossary on page 23.

South Africa in the World

Howzit! My name is Mandisa and I come from South Africa.

Pretoria •
Johannesburg •

• Drakensberg
Mountains

• Khayelitsha

South Africa's place in the world

South Africa is a medium-sized country at the southern tip of the continent of Africa.

I live in Khayelitsha
(say 'ky-ul-it-sha'), a large
township where mostly black
Africans live. It is crowded and
noisy, but it's home!

children play
in the streets
of Khayelitsha
in winter.

People Who Live in South Africa

Black, white, and Asian people live in the main cities.

Around 49 million people live in South Africa. Most are black Africans.

There are also Asians, white people, and people from other African countries.

About two-thirds of South Africans live in cities. The biggest cities are Johannesburg, Cape Town, Durban, and Pretoria. Pretoria is the **capital**.

The rest live in the countryside and work in farming. They tend to be poorer than the people in the cities.

These are Zulu people in the country. The woman is wearing a traditional costume.

South Africa Landscape

South Africa has different **landscapes**. In the center is a high plateau — a large, flat area. In the north is the baking hot Kalahari **Desert**.

The sands of the Kalahari Desert are red.

Around the plateau are hills and mountains. The highest are the Drakensberg Mountains to the east.

The country has a long **coastline** with beaches. The eastern coastline has plenty of rain. The land there is lush and green.

The mountains are covered in snow in winter—perfect for skiing and trekking.

At Home with My Family

My dad is reading a story to my little brother in our living room.

Many people in Khayelitsha and other townships live in **shacks** made from wood and tin.

We have a TV, but most people in townships just listen to the radio.

Some homes in Khayelitsha do not have electricity or **running water**.

We children have to help out at home. I help look after my little brother and sister.

children often fetch water from an outdoor pump.

What We Eat

Mom cooks rice on a small stove.

We mostly eat cheap foods, such as rice and beans. We use a lot of **maize** in our cooking.

My favorite food is chicken. It's our special treat once a week.

12

Richer people in South Africa often eat meat. Barbecues are popular. They are called *braai*.

South Africans also eat foods from different countries, such as Indian curries.

A family enjoys a delicious outdoor barbecue with vegetables.

13

Going to School

South African children start school when they are 5 or 6. When they are 12, they start secondary school. Most parents have to pay for their children to go to school. In the poorest places, there are free schools.

This is my class at school

School usually starts at about 8 A.M. and finishes around 2 P.M.

In most South African schools, children have to wear a school uniform.

There are 40 children in my class. How many children are there in your class?

 # Having Fun

Family is important to all South Africans. We like to spend our free time with close family, such as our aunts, uncles, grandparents, and cousins. I have lots of cousins!

In the townships, people often play soccer in the street.

In South Africa, our favorite sport is soccer. I play nearly every day.

We make our own toys and games. I like rolling old car tires in the street.

My cousin rolls a tire to see how far it will go!

Festivals and Celebrations

Lively christians worship in the province of KwaZulu-Natal.

For us, Christmas is a summer holiday.

Most South Africans are Christians, so Christmas and Easter are important holidays.

There are also Muslims, Hindus, Jews, and people who follow African religions. They celebrate their own **festivals**.

We have several festivals to remember important dates in South African history. Freedom Day is on April 27th, when we celebrate our first **democratic election** held in 1994.

These women celebrate Freedom Day.

19

South Africa has some amazing sights. Around Cape Town, you can learn about big birds and visit beautiful beaches. South Africa has dense forests too.

If you visit Boulders Beach, near Cape Town, you'll see penguins!

At a national park, you can go on a **safari** to see wildlife. You'll see lions, leopards, elephants, and rhinos.

In the townships you can find out about the **local** African **culture** and listen to African music.

An elephant lumbers across the road in Kruger National Park.

Here are some facts about my country!

Fast Facts about South Africa

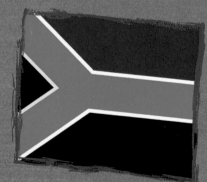

Capital city = South Africa has three capital cities: Pretoria, Cape Town, and Bloemfontein.

Population = 49 million

Currency = the rand

Area = 470,693 square miles (1,219,090 km²)

Languages = 11 main languages. These are spoken by the most people: Afrikaans, English, IsiZulu, Sepedi.

National holiday = Christmas Day

Main religions = Christian, Muslim, Hindu, and African religions

Longest river = Orange River, 1,367 miles (2,200 km)

Highest mountain = Mafadi, 11,319 feet (3,450 m)

Glossary

capital the most important city in a country

coastline the land along a coast

culture the language, food, music, and way of life of a group of people

democratic election when all adults in a country can vote to decide who will rule them

desert a hot, dry area with little rain

festival a special time when people celebrate something

landscape what a place looks like

local to do with the place where you live

maize also known as corn, a grain that is made into flour

running water water that enters buildings in pipes and comes out of taps

safari a trip to see wild animals

shack a small building, usually made from wood or metal

township a town on the edge of a South African city

Further Information

Websites

www.factmonster.com/ipka/A0934644.html

http://kids.nationalgeographic.com/kids/places/find/south-africa

Books

Brownlie Bojang, Alison. *South Africa (Countries in Our World).* Smart Apple Media, 2011

Savery, Annabel. *South Africa (Been There).* Smart Apple Media, 2012

Index